LIE DETECTOR

The Human Body

WRITTEN BY

Simon Holland

ILLUSTRATED BY

Lee Cosgrove

RED
LEMON
PRESS

RED
LEMON
PRESS

First published in Great Britain
by Weldon Owen
Deepdene Lodge
Deepdene Avenue
Dorking RH5 4AT

© 2014 Weldon Owen

All photographs Shutterstock

www.weldonowen.co.uk
www.bonnierpublishing.com

ISBN 978-1-78342-058-2

Printed in China
10 9 8 7 6 5 4 3 2 1

LIE DETECTOR
The Human Body

WRITTEN BY
Simon Holland

ILLUSTRATED BY
Lee Cosgrove

Can you reveal the secrets hidden under your skin, and become a big-brained professor of the Human Body?

When you look at a human, you can only really see what's happening on the outside, and yet there are thousands and thousands of things going on inside the body at any one moment. For hundreds of years, scientists have used different ways to peer inside the body and study its many systems, so that we can all learn about how it really works.

Can you use your head, and get to the bottom of the body's many mysteries? Take a good look at these fun fact or fib questions, and test your brains.

FACT or FIB?

Humans and chimpanzees are actually very similar.

FACT!

DNA is a chemical in the body that holds instructions for how it will grow, develop, work and look. As much as 99 percent of our human DNA is the same as a chimp's DNA. Bananas!

FACT!

Water makes up more than half the weight of a human body. We need this water to get rid of waste from our organs, carry important substances to where they are needed, and to keep the body at the right temperature.

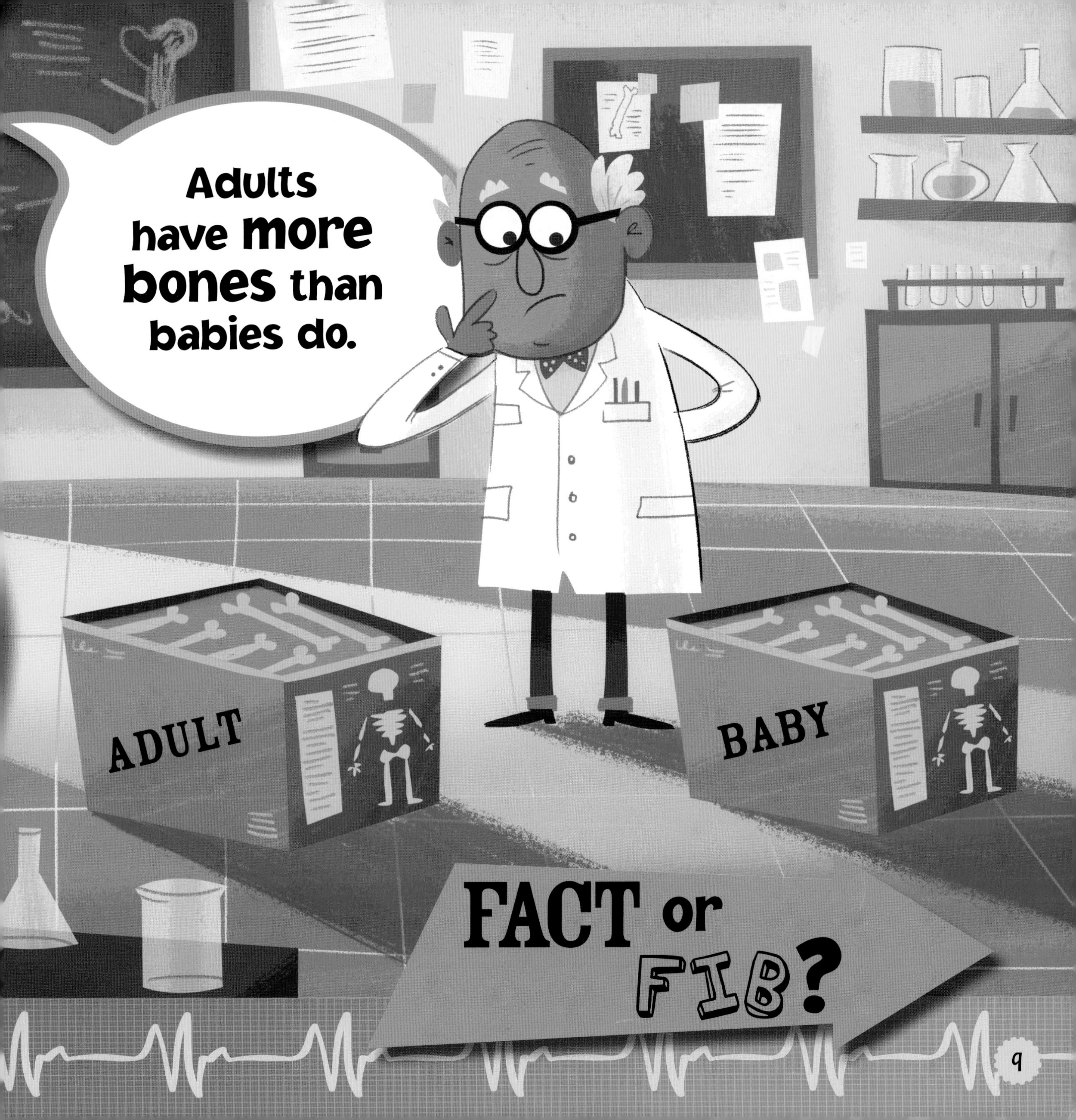
Adults have more bones than babies do.
ADULT
BABY
FACT or FIB?

FIB!

A newborn baby has as many as 300 bones. As its body grows and develops, many of these bones join together. By the time it is fully grown, there will only be 206 bones in its skeleton.

FACT or FIB?

The biggest human **muscle** is in your **bum.**

FACT!

The 'gluteus maximus' is the largest of a group of muscles that make up the rounded shape of the buttocks, or bum! This big muscle helps us to stand upright on our two legs. It also allows us to move our hips and thighs. So come on – let's do the hula!

The smallest bone in the human body is in the little toe.

FACT or FIB?

STAPES

EAR CANAL

FACT or FIB?

Bright spark!

your **brain** can make enough electricity to **power** a **light bulb.**

FACT!

Every time you do something – like move, see, think or hear – electrical signals zap between tiny cells, called neurons, in the brain. These signals carry the information to control your body. When all of these neurons are working together... Ping! Enough electricity is produced to power a light bulb.

LEFT OR RIGHT?

Weirdly, the right-hand side of the brain controls the left half of the body, while the left-hand side of the brain controls the right half of the body.

I feel giddy!

Our eyes see things **upside-down.**

FACT or FIB?

FACT!

Light bounces off objects and then enters our eyes. A picture of the objects then forms at the back of the eyes, but it's the wrong way up. Our brain does the job of turning it the right way round, so that we 'see' the objects as they're meant to look.

Super sleuth

Each time we blink, the eyelids wash the eyes with tears. Along with the eyelashes, these tears get rid of irritating dirt and dust.

BRAIN

PATH OF LIGHT

OPTIC NERVE

Every year, enough air moves in and out of our lungs to fill a hot air balloon.

FACT or FIB?

WINDPIPE

LUNGS

FACT!

Even when resting, fully-grown humans breathe in (and breathe out) about 6 litres of air every minute. That adds up to more than 3 million litres of air each year, which is more than enough to fill an average-sized hot air balloon.

GASSY GOODNESS!

The body needs oxygen to make its cells, tissues and organs work. When we breathe in, air enters our lungs. This is where the vital oxygen gets into our blood.

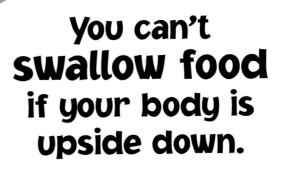

FIB!

Between the mouth and the stomach is a muscly tube called the oesophagus. It squeezes and relaxes in rippling waves to carry food into the stomach. So it doesn't matter if you're sitting down, on a roller coaster or in outer space when you eat – your tummy will still get those snacks!

Humans can replace their teeth regularly, like sharks do.
FACT or FIB?

YOUR TEETH

FIB!

Sharks can regularly lose their teeth and grow new ones, through their whole lives! Humans aren't quite so lucky. Children develop 'milk teeth' (baby teeth), which then fall out to make way for their adult teeth. Most people get 32 of these – but if they fall out or get taken out, there are no more replacements.

Super sleuth

We have four main types of teeth: sharp ones for cutting, pointed ones for tearing, flatter ones for chewing, and – behind the others – bigger teeth for grinding.

FACT or FIB?

In a lifetime, the heart pumps enough blood to fill 50 Olympic-sized swimming pools.

It takes about one minute for a single blood cell to zoom all the way around the body.

FIB!

Actually, it's even more! After 70 years, an average person's heart will have already pumped about 184 million litres of blood around the body. An Olympic-sized swimming pool can hold about 2.5 million litres of liquid, so a human heart could fill at least 75 pools over the course of a lifetime.

HEART PUMPS OUT THE BLOOD

BLOOD FILLS THE HEART

A human **sneeze** can travel faster than a cheetah.

FACT or FIB?

FACT!

The cheetah is the world's fastest animal. It can run at 100 kilometres per hour when chasing its prey. But it's totally out-sprinted by your speeding snot, which you can sneeze out at about 110 kilometres per hour. Just look at it go!

Be good to yourself...

So, what have you learnt from this fun-filled, whistle-stop tour of the human body? You now know that you're similar to a chimp, you're mostly water, your muscly bum helps you to do things on two legs, and that your snot would beat a cheetah in a race. This book has also taught you that you should look after your adult teeth — you won't get any more if they all fall out! But that's not all. On the next page, there's one final challenge to test you.

GUESS WHAT?

Scientists and doctors use special pieces of equipment to see inside the body. X-rays can be passed through the body's tissues to show up hard materials such as bones, and computerized scans can make detailed pictures of our squidgy innards, revealing things that might be causing a health problem. See if you can match these close-up pictures to the correct parts of the human body.

2. What do bones combine to make?

1. Which organs take oxygen from the air?

4. What will you get after your milk teeth go?

3. Can you name the body's control centre?

CHOOSE YOUR ANSWERS FROM THESE BODY BITS:

A. Brain
B. Middle ear
C. Adult teeth
D. Lungs
E. Skeleton

5. Where are these tiny little bones found?

Answers: 1. D, 2. E, 3. A, 4. C, 5. B.

SUPER HUMAN FACTS

BLOOD VESSELS: If the tiny vessels (that carry blood) were all joined up, they would reach to about 150,000 kilometres, or almost four times around the world.

STOMACH POWER: Your stomach squirts acid onto your chomped-up food, which helps to break it down before it goes into your guts for further processing.

STRANDS OF STRENGTH: You've got between 100,000 and 150,000 hairs on your head. If you grew them very long and wove all this hair into a bridge, it could support a couple of elephants!

NOT SO WEE: Over a lifetime, a human could fill about 40,000 1-litre drinks bottles with urine (wee).

SLEEPY PEOPLE: Babies need twice as much sleep as adults do, but even adults spend at least one-third of every year asleep. How lazy!

GLOSSARY

Bone – bones are lengths of hard, whitish tissue that make up the body's framework, the skeleton.

Cell – cells are tiny building blocks that make up all living things.

DNA – a chemical, found inside cells, which carries instructions for how the body should grow, develop and repair itself.

Muscle – a bundle of tissues that contract (squeeze) to move parts of the body.

Neuron – a tiny cell that helps to pass nerve signals around the body.

Optic nerve – carries messages from the eye to the brain, so that we can see.

Organ – a part of the body that does a job. The heart, lungs and skin are all organs.

Oxygen – a gas that we take in, through breathing, to help our cells make energy and do their jobs in the body.

Tissue – cells combine to make tissues of different types – such as the skin, muscles and the different parts of organs.